G000049375

ATHLETICS IN FOCUS

ATHLETICS IN FOCUS

WILF PAISH
AND
TONY DUFFY

LEPUS  BOOKS

ISBN 0 86019 010 2

Filmset and printed in Great Britain by
BAS Printers Limited, Wallop, Hampshire

Contents

Contents

Preface

In compiling this beautiful book the authors aimed to produce a work on track and field athletics that would appeal to the dedicated enthusiast as well as to the mildly interested, to the admirers of human movement whether young or old; in fact a book to browse through to gain something of an insight into the premier sport of the Olympic Games.

It is hoped that readers will find this book different from any other devoted to the sport. The technical matter has been kept to a minimum in order to emphasise the aesthetics of the sport, the emotional and psychological elements and many other peripheral aspects.

It has been a difficult task to select the photographs from the wealth of visual material available. We hope you will find our choice pleasing and enlightening and that, together with the text that introduces each figure, they will provide readers with a glimpse of the 'inside' story of this fascinating sport.

Photographer's Preface

Track and field athletics holds a special fascination for the sports photographer which is difficult to pin-point and define. In essence it concerns the basic simplicity of the sport. Just as in the boxing ring there is no place to hide so too in athletics the competitor's soul is laid bare. His performance is precisely measured and is seen for what it is worth. The stop watch and the tape-measure are remorseless and unforgiving.

Anyone interested in human behaviour cannot but be absorbed in the way an athlete's character is examined during a competition. Some show courage, some unbelievable persistence, some a burning will to win and some crumble under the pressure. All this reflects in the faces of the performers before, during and after the event.

But athletics is primarily about the body — the most magnificent machine ever devised. There is an aesthetic pleasure in watching a finely trained human body exerting itself to capacity or even studying it in repose. The more civilised and luxurious twentieth-century living becomes, the more pleasure the desk-bound and car-bound and generally over-weight Mr. Average derives from watching the elitist corps of top athletes. The Greeks recognised this fact 2,000 years ago and immortalised their heroes in Classical sculpture. Perhaps today's tragedy is that each discipline of track and field is so competitive at the top level that the bodies of many athletes become necessarily distorted by the demands of their particular event. Twenty stone shot-putters and eight stone marathon runners are both equally removed from the Classical Greek ideal.

Seen from the distance of the stands or through the eye of television the top stars of the sports tend to assume the stature of heroes or super-men but they are just ordinary people with the same nerves, fears and frailties as you and I. They were not born great athletes; maybe they were born with natural skills or strength but they had to develop those gifts through back-breaking hours of training. All that goes on behind the scenes in an athlete's life is fascinating. Everything must take second place to training schedules. The normal time-consuming demands of everyday life must be fitted in around the hours spent practising skills or punishing the body in training. Vitamin pills, the right amount of sleep, a balanced diet, the constant

8

nervous tension, the planning, the plotting and the 'psyching-up' all must be coped with and lived with. Nothing comes easy in athletics.

These then are the great appeals of the sport. Its testing of character; its testing of physical fitness and the way of life necessary to accommodate these challenges. These can be captured by the camera and on the rare occasion as in the old adage 'One picture is worth a thousand words'. But there is perhaps a more important contribution that the still camera can make. It can freeze a fraction of a second and capture a moment in time of drama, grace, triumph and tragedy, that are invisible to the naked eye of the observer, and this image can be savoured and analysed. It is an area where the sports specialist can come into his own as he mentally sub-divides each movement or event into its component parts in selecting the shot to take and thus (hopefully!) clicks the shutter at the moment of maximum impact — the long jumper at the apex of his jump, the middle distance field kicking off the final bend, the sprinter hurtling off his blocks like a greyhound, etc.

Sports photographers are often asked what qualities are necessary to obtain a good sports photographs. To my mind there are just two. Firstly, a sympathy for the sport in the sense of an involvement with the athlete's predicament; and secondly reflexes. Given these two factors anyone can take good sports photographs, even with a Box Brownie. The costly paraphernalia of the modern photographer does not of itself ensure good photographs — it is more intended to make him flexible in his coverage of the arena and to get the best quality from the shots he does take. It is no coincidence that the vast majority of successful sports photographers were primarily sports enthusiasts who took up photography as a hobby which later developed into a profession. And believe me, when you are caught up in a cauldron of emotion during an Olympic Games, when all the propaganda, sensation and Nationalism are put on one side and it is man against man in the oldest and purest of all sports, it is hard to think of a better profession to be in.

Tony Duffy

The Authors

It would be difficult to find two men better qualified to produce a text of this nature than Wilfred Paish and Tony Duffy.

Tony Duffy is recognised as one of the world's leading sports photographers, managing to combine an understanding of the sport with highly professional photographic skill. His work can be found in most leading newspapers, in magazines, and on advertisement brochures. In December 1975 he received the Sports Photographer of the Year Award from the Royal Photographic Society of Great Britain and first and second prize in the colour section of the International Sports Photograph of the Year Competition.

Wilfred Paish is a B.A.A.B. national coach, a qualified teacher who has coached international athletes in all of the Olympic track and field events. He has been an official coach at the Commonwealth, European and Olympic Games and has been appointed as an official coach to the British team in Montreal.

ATHLETICS IN FOCUS

Physical Characteristics

Athletics is both the most elaborate and the most simple of all sports. While some events require the sophisticated facilities of the stadia, others are catered for by the national environment. Track and field athletics is a single term used to represent a number of different events for which performers require vastly different physiques, temperaments and skills. In all cases however the competition is of an individual nature: man against man, or against himself or predetermined standards and it is this aspect which appeals to those who like to prove themselves. Provided one is healthy there is an event to suit every variation in size in both sexes. The giant is suited to the heavy throwing events, the linear ectormorph to the high jump and the small and fragile might excel in the distance running events. The two gold medallists from the 1974 Commonwealth Games, Geoff Capes and Ian Thompson, illustrate this clearly.

The following table shows the average heights/weights of competitors at the 1972 Olympic Games and this demonstrates the tremendous variety in physique among track and field athletes.

Event	Men		Women	
	Height	Weight	Height	Weight
Sprints	5 ft 9¼ in.	154 lb	5 ft 6¼ in.	121 lb
Hurdles	6 ft 0½ in.	168 lb	5 ft 5¾ in.	127 lb
High Jump	6 ft 2 in.	185 lb	5 ft 10 in.	141 lb
Long Jump	6 ft 0 in.	164 lb	5 ft 6¼ in.	121 lb
Shot	6 ft 3¾ in.	270 lb	5 ft 9 in.	180 lb
Discus	6 ft 3½ in.	243 lb	5 ft 10 in.	181 lb
Javelin	6 ft 0 in.	211 lb	5 ft 8 in.	147 lb

Figs 1 and 2 Ian Thompson, England marathon runner, and (*opposite*) Geoff Capes (G.B.), shot putter.

Competition

Fig. 3 (*below*) The 1972 Olympic 100 metres won by Renate Stecher (East Germany) from Raelene Boyle (Australia). The winner is obvious; less obvious is the result for third place, which was awarded to No. 66 after the photograph was taken. The photo-finish equipment is in the foreground.

Competition in athletics is of two kinds; what may be termed instant and non-instant. The instant, direct type can be seen in any running event when both performer and spectator are immediately aware of the result, or the photo-finish equipment determines the order when the finish is close.

The field events involve the performer in direct competition but the results are not instant. The tape measure is the arbitrator and the result is not known until the last person has taken the final attempt.

The vertical jumps produce a slightly different type of competition because competitors are involved in a process of elimination; based on the ability to clear a bar which is raised progressively. It might be termed 'survival of the fittest'.

Fig. 4 (*opposite*) Bob Beamon (U.S.A.) wins the 1968 Olympic Long Jump in Mexico City. The greatest athletic feat to date! Can it ever be equalled at sea-level?

In winning this event Beamon clearly illustrates the variety of types of competition involved in a single jump. By long jumping 8·90 m (29 ft 2½ in.) he obviously achieved a personal standard, proved his superiority over all other jumpers in the competition, and shattered the world record, an ever changing standard. With many athletes, particularly the lesser mortals, it is the 'indirect' competition which has the most significant meaning: the ability to achieve a club, school or national standard, while even to come last in a competition, where one beats one's own personal best, is still a good measure of success.

The Event Structure

The chart below illustrates that the sport is divided into two distinct categories. The track events embrace those where the performer runs a set distance, either on the straight or around the circular track, sometimes carrying a baton, passed from runner to runner, and sometimes clearing obstacles like hurdles. The field events represent the jumping and throwing competitions, usually held in the centre of the arena, or at adjacent areas to the track.

Some competitions combine a number of events together as in the decathlon (ten events) for men and the pentathlon (five events) which is primarily for women.

The structure also includes marathon running and race walking, where the bulk of the event takes place outside the stadium on the surrounding roads. The marathon is always assured a permanent place in the Olympic programme and is usually the final event of the Games, but the future of the walking events is under close review.

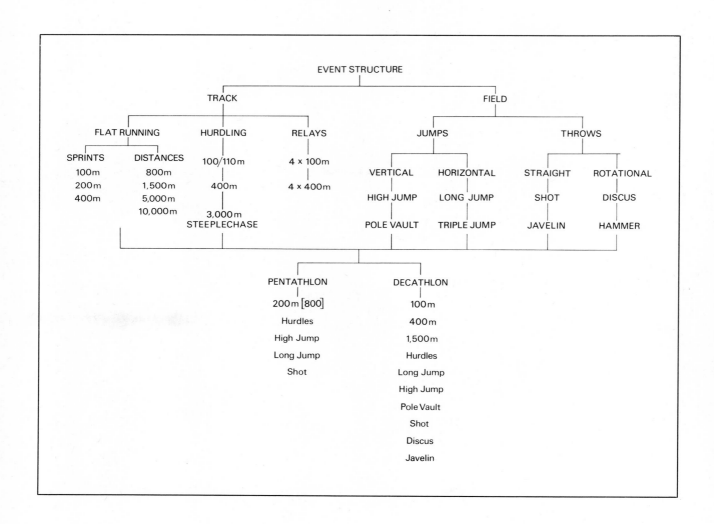

Sprinting

Fig. 5 The relaxed, powerful stride of the 1972 Olympic 200 and 100 metres champion, Valeriy Borzov, No. 932. Notice the complete absence of tension from the neck when compared with No. 256.

Sprinting can be defined as full speed running for the complete duration of the race. Because of the strenuous nature of the exercise, the distance is restricted to 400 metres or less (i.e. 100 metres and 200 metres).

Speed, over a distance, is determined by the rate of striding (cadency) and stride length. There is obviously an optimum value for both, but all sprinters aim to achieve as long a stride as possible without allowing the cadency to drop.

Fig. 6 (*below*) 100 metres. West German championships 1972.

The sprinter, who wishes to reach peak speed as quickly as possible, performs very precise movements in response to the starter's commands of 'on your marks' and 'set'. He usually adopts a crouched position, employing the use of starting blocks (ref. figs. 5/90). The report of the gun, fired by the starter (ref. fig. 86) sets up an almost reflex pattern of movements.

However, the true mettle of a sprinter is not judged by who can leave the starting line first, but by who reaches the finishing line first. The great sprinter is one who performs the most work while the foot is in contact with the track surface. In a top-class 100 metre race for men, the foot contacts the ground about 40 times, in a period of approximately ten seconds, so producing an average stride length of about 2·5 m (7 ft 9 in.).

Fig. 7 (*opposite*)   Irena Szewinska *née* Kirzenstein (Poland).

If asked to select the female athlete of this decade, I would vote for this woman. In 1964 she won silver medals in the Olympic long jump and 200 metres, and in 1974 she set a world record for the 400 metres. In the years between these achievements she studied at university and produced a family.

The 400 metres event is a very demanding one, which pushes the athlete close to the physiological limits in terms of oxygen consumption. By systematic conditioning, the sprinter develops a callousness towards fatigue and can will the body to continue when all else is compelling it to retire. This situation is particularly in evidence in the closing stages of the race, hence the 400 metres runner must know how to apportion effort.

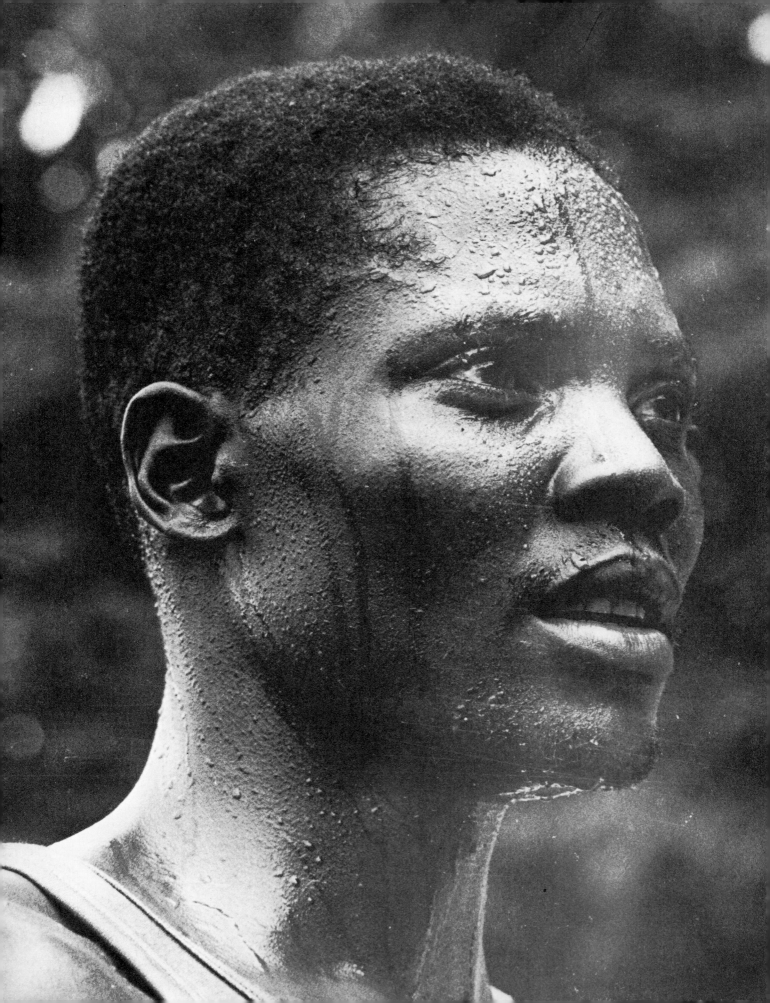

Middle Distance

Fig. 8 Middle distance running is all about hard work, witness this photograph of the face of Ben Jipcho (Kenya).

The middle distance events comprise the flat races held around the circular track: the 800 metres, 1,500 metres, 5,000 metres and 10,000 metres. These are the events listed in the Olympic programme, which fails to recognise the 'magic mile'.

For many years the possibility of a mile run in four minutes, captured the interests of track enthusiasts. The dream was realised on May 6th, 1954 when Roger Bannister broke the barrier for the first time (fig. 74). Such a feat is now commonplace; which is just a measure of progress.

In the middle distance events the body has to work efficiently when the vital fuels for this type of work are only barely adequate. During training, the runner must frequently place himself in this stressed condition, so that the mind, the heart, the lungs and the muscles recognise fatigue, overcome it, and still continue to work. The middle distance runner will often train for an average of 100 miles each week of the year with long, relaxed, runs of about 20 miles duration, and varying amounts of fast intermittent running over short distances.

Fig. 9 Brendan Foster (Great Britain), European 5,000 metres champion and world record holder for 2 miles. Brendan first made his mark as a 1,500 metres runner in the Commonwealth Games of 1970. Lack of basic speed caused him to move up in distance, running both the 5,000 and 10,000 metres. He will certainly start as one of the pre-race favourites for the 1976 5,000 and/or 10,000 metres.

Brendan, an ex-teacher, is now recreation officer for Gateshead. Wherever he runs his Tyneside supporters follow him with their chorus of 'Awey big Bren'.

Fig. 10 (*pages 24/25*) Taken during a race staged at the English Association Football Cup final at the Wembley Stadium 1974, David Bedford leads a star-studded field which includes No. 1 Ian Stewart, Emiel Puttemans at his shoulder and Tony Simmons No. 4.

Great Britain also has a strong tradition in this group of events. Shrubb, George, Wooderson, Bannister, Pirie, Chattaway, Ibbotson, Bedford and Foster have all been world record holders, with tremendous crowd pulling potential, but no other athlete, in recent years, has quite captured the respect of the crowd like David Bedford. Bedford, who is the present record holder for 10,000 metres, has not lived up to expectation in major events like the Olympic Games. It is often said that he is a world beater but not a medallist. One can hope that his current injury will repair in time to prove his critics wrong.

Middle Distance

Fig. 11 To date a number of superb middle distance runners have emerged from East Africa, but none have quite captured the imagination like Filbert Bayi, photographed here during the 1971 Commonwealth Games in Christchurch.

Bayi was first noticed when finishing well down in a top-class field, having led the race, during the early stages, at what was considered a suicidal pace. The pundits were heard saying, 'If only someone could teach him to run', 'If only he could be taught tactics'. To their surprise, in later races, instead of fading during the final stages of a race, he just kept on going. The result was a gold medal in the Commonwealth Games of 1974 with a new record for the 1,500 metres of 3 mins 32·2 secs. Bayi led from 'gun to tape' taking with him four other runners, who now appear in the top ten for the best ever performances for this, the metric mile.

It must be recognised that performances like this do not stem from natural ability alone. Such ability is nurtured carefully with the aid of the environment, diet and hard work. But the saying 'Tha' can't put in what God left out', attributed to a famous Yorkshire cricketer, must remain true for this, as well as any other sport.

Middle Distance

Fig. 12 A field during an international 800 metres event for women. The 800 metres is now almost recognised as a sprint, a fact emphasised by observing that only one foot, from the whole group in the photograph, is fully in contact with the ground. Recent evidence suggests that future world record holders for this event will come from sprinters who have modified their training to cope with the extra distance.

Number 98 is Lillian Board, who won an Olympic medal in 1968 in the 400 metres, but who died tragically in 1972 from cancer.

Number 313 is Vera Nikolic (Yugoslavia) favourite to win the 1968, 800 metres event. Vera broke down during the event with mental exhaustion, emphasising that athletes are not just physiological machines. It is the psychological which can mean the difference between defeat or victory.

Middle Distance

Fig. 13 Lasse Viren, taken after the 1972 Olympic 5,000 metres. Viren is a typical example of the new Finnish School of middle distance running.

Finland, with a population the same size as greater London, has a history of producing great middle distance stars like Paavo Nurmi, whose haul of Olympic medals during 1920—8 is a record.

During the period 1948—70 Finland's claims to success declined, then, in 1970, a new administrative structure set about the task of recapturing the old glory. Training ideas, based on the principles of Arthur Lydiard, the famed New Zealand coach, began the resurgence. A study of the other training variables such as environment, diet, altitude training etc., provided the scientific basis necessary for regaining their supremacy. Their battles with the East African nations, on the running track at the next Olympic Games, will certainly provide one of the highlights of 1976.

Number 1005 is Steve Prefontaine, potentially one of the greatest distance runners from the U.S.A. who was tragically killed in a car accident in 1975.

Harrier Running

Fig. 14 The English 'National' cross country championships. The numbers on the vests indicate the size of the field. In this race, the mediocre can rub shoulders with the elite, even if it is only at the start!

England has considerable depth of performance in the distance events which is a direct result of the strong harrier traditions. Indeed, the development of track and field athletics in the United Kingdom, owes its success to the harrier clubs and their officials. Unfortunately, such a tradition could eventually restrict the full development of the sport. The 'harrier philosophy' does not really comply with the demands of the field event athletes. The lengthy competitive fixture list encourages good athletes to compete for 52 weeks of the year; a situation not conducive towards 'peaking' for an Olympic Games.

Like steeplechasing, the harrier tradition could derive from hunting on horseback. The early development of the sport is associated with games like 'fox and hounds', 'paper chasing' etc., working-class versions of the rich men's sports.

The Marathon

Fig. 15 Ron Hill, one of Britain's most successful marathon runners, illustrates the relaxed style necessary to complete the full course of 26 miles 385 yards.

The length of the race, originally chosen as 26 miles, represented the distance supposedly run by Pheidippides in 490 B.C. from Marathon to Athens, to convey the news that the Greeks had destroyed the Persian army. In the first modern Olympics in 1896 the race was run over the route believed to have been taken by Pheidippides, and fortune aided the Greeks who filled the first three places of this inaugural race.

When the Olympic Games came to London in 1908, the organisers felt that a lap of the stadium, in view of the reigning monarch, was a fitting end to such a test of endurance. Hence the 385 yards was added.

In this picture Ron Hill is wearing a metallised string vest to help keep the body cool. During a race, feeding and sponging stations are placed along the route so that athletes can take a drink, which aids the delicate fluid/salt balance, and sponge down with cool water.

The Marathon

Fig. 16 (*opposite*) Frank Shorter (U.S.A.) examines his blistered feet after the 1972 Olympic marathon knowing that his efforts have been rewarded by a gold medal.

Blistered feet cause many marathon runners to retire from a race. The marathon lasts for over two hours, during which the feet strike the road some 28,000 times and the inevitable build up of heat in the shoe causes the blisters.

Marathon runners are frail even though they have extreme powers of endurance. Considerable thought is given to the planning of their training, racing and pre-race diet. Most marathon runners employ the carbohydrate loading system: the starvation of carbohydrates for a period prior to a race, followed by a period of carbohydrate saturation directly before.

Where Next?

Fig. 17 (*below*) Oxygen is used to aid the recovery of distressed athletes after performing at a high altitude.

Reading through the list of venues for the Olympic Games, certain nations have most unsuitable climates for sport and one wonders whether the performance of the athlete is ever considered when making the selection.

The choice for 1968 was Mexico City, at an altitude of 7,500 feet. The 'power' event athletes were more than happy, but physiologists feared for the well-being of distance runners. Research into performance at altitude, made necessary by this choice of venue, suggested that athletes could enhance their performances at sea-level by training at altitude for an extended period prior to a race. It was also established that acclimatisation could not equal the advantage which an athlete has by being born and nurtured at altitude. While pre-Olympic training at altitude will now become part of a nation's preparation for the Games, more middle distance athletes will continue to emerge from the high altitude countries like East Africa.

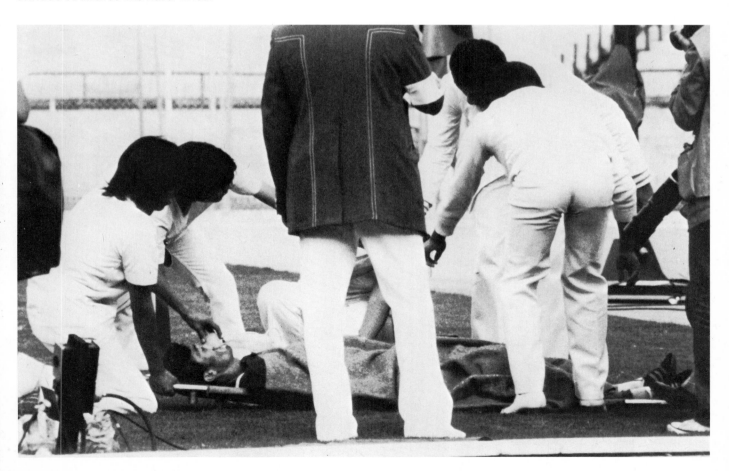

Steeplechase

Fig. 18 Part of the field going over the water jump at the 1972 Olympic Games. The clearance technique of No. 271 is superb when compared with that of No. 572 who is wasting time in the air.

Fig. 19 (*opposite*) A fish-eye shot of the water jump at the Crystal Palace, which clearly illustrates the technique.

Before the race came under the close specifications of today's rules, the steeplechase was considered the 'circus' event to amuse the crowds. Water jumps were often constructed to be so difficult that the runner invariably emerged drenched with water and covered with mud. Today, it would be impossible still for an athlete to fully clear the whole obstacle, as a horse might, but the athlete emerges from the water with only one foot wet.

With the less demanding hurdle, as in fig. 20, the athlete clears it in a manner similar to that shown in fig. 22.

Steeplechase

Fig. 20 A famous Kenyan trio: No. 272 Amos Biwott, No. 267 Ben Jipcho (fig. 8) and Kipchoge Keino, the 1968 Olympic 1,500 metres champion and the 1972 Olympic steeplechase champion. None of them show any expertise in clearing the hurdle, but they can certainly run fast between them!

It is suggested that the event owes its origin to 'first back to a local landmark', a race practised by gentlemen after a day's hunting; the church 'steeple' being a local landmark visible for miles. The first true indications of its history came in 1850 at Oxford when the chance comment 'I would rather run round that course on foot than mount that camel' (referring to a horse) was taken up as a challenge.

The modern event covers 3,000 metres of the circular track with 28 hurdles, each 91·5 cms (3 ft) high, and seven water jumps, of the same height, followed by a trough of water.

Basically, the event calls for a good middle distance runner who has the courage and ability to clear the formidable barriers when fatigued.

Hurdling

Fig. 21 Guenther Nickel (West Germany) shows the balancing action of the arms which helps him to run in the very narrow 'tunnel'.

The high hurdles race follows approximately the same pattern as its flat, sprint, equivalent. The rules permit the runner to knock down all of the hurdles (provided some attempt is made to clear them), although the effect on speed would be disastrous. The 'tunnel' does not permit much space for stride adjustment and loss of balance.

Fig. 22 (*pages 44/45*) Berwyn Price (G.B.) on the way to winning a gold medal in the 1973 Universiad held in Moscow. Berwyn, nearest the camera, appears to be in unison with all of his rivals as they 'straddle' the hurdle.

Hurdlers are often called 'rhythm sprinters', suggesting that they are sprinters and that the ten, equally spaced hurdles, impose a certain rhythm.

The sprint hurdle (110 metres for men, 100 metres for women) is usually an eight plus three rhythm, the athletes taking eight strides to the first hurdle, with three strides to cover the interval between hurdles. The 400 metres hurdles race does not impose quite such a precise rhythm.

The high hurdler must be able to sprint over the obstacles, which would be impossible without modifying the basic sprinting style. The leap, to accommodate the hurdle, entails a recovery of the trailing leg to the side of the body.

Hurdling

Fig. 23 Guenther Nickel winning the 1972 West German championships. This picture clearly illustrates the 'ups and downs' of the event. It captures athletes on the way 'up' to clear the hurdle as can be seen in the bent leg 'pick-up' of Adolf Heine (No. 1080). One can see Nickel on the way 'down', emphasising the high trailing leg aiding the pivot across the hurdle, and the subsequent stride pattern.

Some hurdles remain upright, some have been toppled but the Junghans timing mechanism will decide who is on top.

Hurdling

Fig. 24 It looks as if No. 2, John Sherwood, bronze medallist in the 1968 Olympic Games, is about to take the same hurdle as David Hemery, gold medallist in the same event. This is not the case however, as, like the 400 metres flat, this race is run in lanes, with the hurdles staggered so that they are the same distance apart for each athlete.

The event was termed the 'man killer', as prior to 1964, it usually attracted slow, high hurdlers or slow, 400 metres flat men. Nowadays, women do the event without any undue discomfort, which reflects our progress in training ideas.

The 400 metres hurdler has a unique problem. When fresh it is possible for most athletes to take 13 strides, or less, between each hurdle. This would be impossible in the closing stages when fatigue sets in, so they have to 'change down'. For example, John Akii Bua (Uganda), gold medallist in the 1972 Games, used 13 strides to the fifth hurdle, changed to 14 for the next three hurdles and concluded the race using a 15 stride rhythm.

Relays

Fig. 25 Andrea Lynch (G.B.) runs away from Judy Vernon, after having received the baton during a sprint relay. This excellent picture shows how the running strides of the two athletes must be 'matched' for an efficient exchange. The efficiency of the exchange is usually a matter of practice, during which athletes learn to understand each other, and select 'cue' marks to aid the blend.

A relay is a contest between two, or more, teams of runners, who cover the same distance. The Olympic committee recognise the 4 × 100 metres and the 4 × 400 metres, with the athletes exchanging a baton. In this type of race it must be remembered that it is always the 'baton' which wins the race.

Relays probably represent an attempt, on the part of officialdom, to create a team atmosphere in what is essentially an individual sport. If the Olympic Games are to survive, it will be necessary to restrict the number of participants and it may well be that the team events, including the athletic relays, will be abolished.

Relays

Fig. 26 Sharon Colyear (G.B.) passes the baton to Anita Neal, using the fairly common 'up sweep' method. The baton must be exchanged within a twenty metres zone, using hand to hand contact on the baton. In the sprint relay it is usual for the first and third runners to carry the baton in the right hand, thus saving distance on the bends, and for the second and fourth runners to receive and carry in their left hands. As can be seen from the photograph, the exchange is non-visual as far as the receiver is concerned. The placing of the baton is the responsibility of the incoming runner, and the position of the exchange, relative to the zone, mainly that of the outgoing runner. A system of check marks aid the outgoing runner, with an audible call from the incoming runner should this prove inaccurate. In an emergency the outgoing runner might have to 'run on the spot' to keep the exchange legal.

Fig. 27 (*pages 54/55*) The final exchange involving West Germany, Kenya, Poland, Great Britain and France, during the final of the 1972 Olympic 4 × 400 metres relay.

The 400 metres relay is a visual exchange; the outgoing runner must look for the baton, and judge the speed of the incoming runner, which can vary considerably due to fatigue. West Germany is just passing the baton. Poland and G.B. have received the baton and are in the process of changing the hand-hold from left for receive, to right for carry.

This event produced a silver medal for Great Britain whose team included David Jenkins as its only specialist 400 metres runner, together with two 400 metre hurdlers and one 200 metres runner.

Race Walking

Fig. 28 Bernd Kannenberg is seen here winning the 1972 Olympic Games, 50 kilometres walk. He led from almost start to finish and doing so beat his rivals by over two minutes.

Race walking has many critics who say that it is impossible to keep the rule of unbroken contact with the ground. Walkers who 'lift' are no more guilty of breaking the rules than athletes who accept payments or who take drugs.

Walking was first introduced to the Olympic Games, in the form of a 50 kilometres walk, in 1932. The 20 kilometres walk first appeared in 1956 and will now be the only event held in the 1976 Olympics.

Shot Putting

Fig. 29 Randy Matson (U.S.A.) 1968 Olympic Champion and world record holder, during one of the final international meetings at the White City, London.

Shot putting is an event where skill and strength are matched against an object shaped like a cannonball. The weights of the ball varies according to age and sex: 7·25 kilo (16 lb) for adult men and 4 kilo (8 lb 13 oz) for women. It is a competition for distance thrown with the performer required to remain within a circle, measuring 2·135 m (7 ft) in diameter, for the entire throwing movement.

The event attracts the big, strong extrovert person. It appears that an improvement in distance is often related to an increase in physique. Statistics taken from the last four Olympic Games indicate that the average weight of a thrower is increasing by about 10 lb per Olympiad and it is suggested that this gain is associated with a group of hormone drugs known as the anabolic steroids. The fact is recognised by the controlling bodies, who are attempting to find a test to detect these drugs. Researchers are having problems with the test, because the drugs are associated with testosterone, the male sex hormone, which is produced naturally in the body. However, it must be accepted that one cannot disturb the delicate hormonal balance of the body without the risk of long-term side-effects.

A

B

C

D

Shot Putting

Figs 30a–g Brian Oldfield, the professional world record holder, performs his rather unusual spiral movement. Brian Oldfield, who was a member of the 1972 USA Olympic team, decided to join the I.T.A. professional troupe, so robbing future Olympics of a colourful personality.

The distance thrown is mainly dependent upon the speed of release and, over the years, athletes have experimented with ways in which to improve this factor. This style is a fairly recent result of experimentation. At present, most athletes prefer to use a modified O'Brien technique, as shown in figs 29, 31, 32 and 33, named after the athlete who first introduced the style.

Balance is a key feature of the event. Loss of balance will prevent the big athlete from exerting the maximum pushing force necessary to propel the shot a long way. Under the present rules, the rotational style has inherent balance problems, although it is likely that every adaptable athlete will master these in time.

E

F

G

Shot Putting

Fig. 31 Marianne Adam (East Germany) current world record holder is pictured here during an 'O'Brien shift', a glide backwards across the circle. Adam is just one of a group of Eastern European women who have dominated this event for over 20 years.

Critics of the sport suggest that shot putting is not very feminine. Another decade of emancipation might silence them. It is an event which appeals to the big, explosive woman who would not be happy gracing the courts of Wimbledon. Women perform the event in an identical manner to men, use the same rules for competition and their records are on a par. The only significant difference is the weight of the shot.

Fig. 32 George Woods (U.S.A.) a world record holder, conveys the true meaning of the event. Like Geoff Capes (fig. 2) he is a man with excellent physique and complete mastery of the skills involved. The legs and arms reflect many hours of strength training.

The picture illustrates the rotational nature of even this conventional technique. The propelling force is initiated by the right leg (for right-handed throwers). Its action forces the hips and chest square to the front, so that the fast, acting arm can take over the movement. Mechanically speaking, the slow muscles act first, with the faster, yet weaker muscles, adding their power later in the movement. The correct interplay of the muscles produces the greatest speed of release.

Shot Putting

Fig. 33 Mike Winch (G.B.) admires the idol of most shot putters, Al Feuerbach (U.S.A.). Feuerbach, at a height of 186 cms and a weight of 114 kilo, is relatively small when compared with some giants in this event, but his excellent technique more than compensates for this, to make him a world record holder.

It is an excellent action shot. The position of the fingers reflect their final 'flipping' action, while the position of the shot indicates a high release. Assuming a constant launching force and angle of trajectory, the shot will travel further the higher it is released. The range improvement, per foot height, is about 11 in. (30 cms : 27 cms). This further indicates the advantage that a tall person has over a short one in this event.

Discus Throwing

Fig. 34 The photographer recreates the discobolus pose by Myron, using Peter Gabbett, international decathlete, as a model.

Discus throwing is the classic athletic event with more writings and artistic impressions to its credit than any other. The pose reflects the artist's impression rather than a factual depiction of an ancient technique. However, it is certain that Myron's statue influenced the modern development of the sport. In the early, modern, Olympic Games there were two discus competitions: a 'free-style' event with techniques similar to those used today; and a 'classic' event where the thrower adopted a Myron-like pose on top of a raised pedestal (*balbis*). The classic style imposed restrictions, producing lower levels of performance, so its life as an Olympic event was short-lived.

The event, as it is performed today, calls for the thrower to race across a circle, measuring 2·50 m (8 ft 2$\frac{1}{2}$ in.) in diameter, and hurl a saucer-shaped object. The weight of the discus varies according to age and sex: a 2 kilo discus for men and a 1 kilo for women.

Discus Throwing

Fig. 35 Faina Melnik (U.S.S.R.) 1972 Olympic champion, world record holder and probably the greatest female thrower of all time. Melnik, at the time of writing, is consistently three metres ahead of her nearest rivals.

A discus thrower needs the strength of Milo and the poise of the ballet dancer, a feature well in evidence in this picture. Melnik is about to drive across the circle, using a running rotational turn, to produce the initial speed necessary for long throws.

Discus Throwing

Fig. 36 Melnik captured in the pose just before the final arm action. This photograph together with fig. 35 clearly illustrate the true nature of the event.

The 'bowed' effect of the back is produced by the need for torque, and is brought about by the right leg having driven the hips and shoulders ahead of the discus. The movement is completed by a fast arm action, as the weight passes over the front foot, which acts as a brace.

Discus Throwing

Fig. 37 Carol Martin, Canada, sends the 1 kilo discus spinning into orbit.

Discus throwing is a long arm slinging action. The discus is not gripped in any way; it is merely kept pressed against the end of the fingers by centrifugal force, set up by the rotational nature of the event. At release, the discus spins automatically away from the first finger. It is this gyroscopic spinning action which stabilises the flight and makes the discus a better airfoil. The discus can be made to spin faster than 300 r.p.m. which, in theory, could produce a 'magnus' lifting effect. Manufacturers now exploit this feature and produce discoi with most of the weight towards the metal rim, which tends to aid the 'flywheel' spinning action.

Javelin Throwing

Fig. 38 Concentration captured on the face of Ruth Fuchs, Olympic champion 1972 and world record holder, from East Germany. The pose clearly illustrates the rotational nature of the event.

The javelin throw is the most beautiful and probably the oldest throwing event. Early Greek pottery depicts spear throwers in similar poses suggesting that this is an event that has been handed down by our spear-throwing ancestors.

Unlike all of the other throws, it is not restricted by a circle. It is rather like a horizontal jumping event, where the run is terminated by a throw instead of a jump.

To launch a javelin over 90 m (300 ft) requires great skill and timing, and throwers reach release speeds of 30 m/sec (100 ft/sec). Further improvements on this level will make the event difficult to contain in the conventional stadium. As athletics is a spectator sport, stringent safety precautions must be observed. A rotational style, developed in Spain during the fifties, broke world records but would have cleared the stands of people. Its supporters could not predict its flight direction!

Javelin Throwing

Fig. 39 Tessa Sanderson (G.B.) caught in a warrior-like pose; the hunter about to capture the prey.

Most javelin throwers take an approach run over 30 m (100 ft), before releasing the javelin, the size of which, as in all throwing events, varies with age and sex. Rules also control its flight path and release point.

Fig. 40 (*right*) Klaus Wolferman, the 1972 Olympic champion. Wolferman defeated the Russian favourite Janis Lusis (fig. 41) the reigning Olympic champion, by a mere 2 cms. In Munich 1972, electronic measuring equipment was used for the first time. It seems doubtful whether elaborate measuring equipment can compensate for the human error, as in identifying the correct landing mark, to this degree of accuracy.

Wolferman is shown here during the transition phase of the throw, where the javelin is withdrawn to a position behind the body. Perfect poise and control and tremendous mobility of the trunk and shoulders are necessary. Here the spring is being coiled ready to explode in the final throwing action.

Javelin Throwing

Fig. 41 Janis Lusis
(U.S.S.R.) recognised as the
greatest thrower of all time.
He won the 1968 Olympic
title, was third in the 1964
Games and second in the 19
Olympics. His achievements
also include four European
titles.

The 1968 final was the
epitomy of competition.
Lusis, the favourite to win,
was in fourth position before
the final throw of the competition. The crowd was sile
as Lusis started his final
approach, which he checked
in mid air before release, thu
prolonging the suspense. Th
re-run was dramatic, the
javelin soared into the air an
landed at 90 m 10 cms (295
7 in.), a new Olympic record

The picture illustrates an
excellent athletic build. Mos
javelin throwers are good all
round athletes and many hav
competed, with distinction,
as decathletes. The table
(*opposite*) indicates how th
javelin throwers are misfits i
the throws group. The
statistics are taken from a
1968 Olympic Games surve

Fig. 42 The contorted face of Charlie Clover (Great Britain), 1974 Commonwealth Champion and a junior world record holder.

Javelin throwers are more a product of 'nature' than 'nurture', in that a fast throwing arm is a pre-requisite. Most world class throwers can hurl the 800 gms javelin over 60 m (200 ft approx.) from a standing position, using the arm alone.

The 'bow' action as seen in fig. 41 is caused by the driving action of the right leg and hip. The bracing action of the left side, which helps to speed up the rotation in the right side, is in evidence here.

Event	Height		Weight	
Shot	6 ft 3½ in.	(192 cms)	270 lb	(123 kg)
Discus	6 ft 4 in.	(193 cms)	243 lb	(110 kg)
Hammer	6 ft 1½ in.	(188 cms)	232 lb	(105 kg)
Javelin	6 ft 0 in.	(184 cms)	185 lb	(84 kg)

High Jumping

Fig. 43 Reynaldo Brown (U.S.A.) approaches the zenith of a straddle style high jump. Brown was only 17 years of age when he competed in the 1968 Olympic Games.

Over the years the changing bar clearance styles have been the main focus of attention in the high jump. Such changes have nearly always brought new records. In the early days of high jumping, competitors had to land on grass, so safety factors restricted the style to one where the performer could land feet first, i.e. a straight jump or a scissors style. Soft sand landing areas brought the Eastern Cut-Off introduced by Mike Sweeny in about 1895, and the Western Roll developed by George Horine in 1912. The straddle style was first introduced by Dave Albritton in 1936 and this style dominated the international scene until 1968, when Fosbury demonstrated his flop style and won the Olympic title. What better way to demonstrate the success of a new style, but it could not have developed without the aid of the technologists who provided safe landing beds.

The development of the event is almost entirely due to the Americans but the effect of the Russian raised shoe cannot be ignored.

Fig. 44 Reynaldo Brown (U.S.A.) executes a straddle take-off. With the straddle style the take-off foot is nearest the bar; the approach run is at about 30 degrees to the uprights. The final strides of the run must be on the heels so most jumpers wear heel spikes, which can be seen in this picture.

Spring is the essential quality of a high jumper and some men can direct enough power, through a single leg, to throw them into orbit over 2·15 m (7 ft). While most of the lifting force is derived from the extension of the take-off leg, the free leg and arms also contribute.

The position of take-off is precise. It must be such that the legs (the most difficult part of the body to clear) cross the low point of the bar (the centre).

Fig. 45 Rosemarie Witschas (East Germany) world record
holder, looks good from almost any angle. She is in fact about to
clear the trailing leg, as she rotates to land on her back, in a bed of
soft foam. The clearance of the trailing leg is one of the major
problems facing the straddle jumper.

Fig. 46 The originator of the Fosbury style, Dick Fosbury, U.S.A., in a light hearted mood at the peak of a jump. Within a short space of time this style had given high jumping a new dimension. It brought an element of fun into the event which the very precise, demanding, skills of the straddle jump had precluded.

As fig. 48 shows, it is not a backwards jump. The take-off is similar to the old scissors style with the foot furthest from the bar. In other respects it is like a long jump when one looks at the free leg action.

Fig. 47 The prospect of a 'happy landing' for Val Harrison (Great Britain).

In its early days the Fosbury flop had many critics. They were supported by pseudo-medics who tried to get the style banned. If the facilities are suitable then the jump is NOT dangerous, so facilities should be improved rather than a successful style of high jumping condemned.

As can be seen from the photograph, the landing is high up on the back, a vulnerable area unless adequately protected.

Fig. 48 The current world record holder, Dwight Stones (U.S.A.) soon after leaving the ground.

The problem facing the 'flopper' is one of gaining rotation, about the vertical axis of the body, in order to pass over the bar on the back. All 'floppers' use a curved approach run to aid the movement. Further rotation is obtained from an eccentric thrust at take-off and a concentric movement of the free leg. Both are in evidence in this photograph.

Photographer's Choice

Fig. 49 Debbie Brill (Canada) in a beautiful suspended, pose, about to clear the bar, with her version of the Fosbury flop, during the 1972 Olympic Games. Debbie aptly terms her style the 'Brill bend'!

Tony Duffy

Fig. 50 Start shot—Women. Women in sport, and athletics in particular, have been much maligned in the past as eccentrics or as muscular freaks. Nothing is further from the truth. Their events are every bit as competitive as the men's, and their standard rate of improvement is rising at a faster rate as more girls take up the sport and the 'emancipation' of the female sex gathers pace. At the top level the girls can add an ingredient missing from the men's events which can be summed up in one word—grace. I took this start shot of Donna Murray in my studio in order to isolate the figure in the explosive start of a sprinter so that the eye is not distracted from the fantastic line and grace of a top woman athlete. This is one instance where the lens can capture a moment that the naked eye cannot fully register.

Tony Duffy

Fig. 51 (*below*) Explosion shot. Apart from what might be called 'straight' no-gimmick photography, there are certain photographic techniques which I feel may help to say something about the sport. Not everyone will agree with this but at least it may produce a topic for discussion. This technique is known as an 'explosion' shot and is achieved with a zoom lens which is zoomed-in at the same time as the shutter is pressed. It is very much a hit or miss affair. This shot was taken during the steeplechase event at the Olympics.

Tony Duffy

Fig. 52 (*opposite*) Start shot — Men. Athletics is all about competition and for me this photo says 'competition'. Taken during a heat of the 100 m during the 1972 Olympics it shows the different nationalities all reacting to the starter's pistol, with determination mirrored on every face. No room here for the half-hearted or the uncommitted.

Tony Duffy

Fig. 53 (*opposite*)   Javelin Girl. Coloured athletes are probably the most naturally gifted of all athletic groups in track and field. For me this photo is simply — 'Black Power' — but not in the political sense. The enjoyment of the girl, Tessa Sanderson, is self-evident, so too is the 100% effort and her natural rhythm and co-ordination.

Tony Duffy

Fig. 54 (*below*)   An impression shot effect, with Andrea Lynch (Great Britain) European silver medallist for the 100 metres, in focus.

Tony Duffy

Long Jump

Fig. 55 Randy Williams (U.S.A.) during the leap of 8 m 24 cm (27 ft 0 in.) which gave him the 1972 Olympic title. It seems almost mediocre when compared with Beamon's jump (fig. 4) in 1968.

The long jump is a compromise for the athlete. The jumper would like to have the best of two worlds, i.e. maximum vertical lift and horizontal speed. The combination of the qualities of the fastest sprinter in the world, and the highest jumper could possibly achieve a long jump of over 11 m (36 ft). But if the jumper approached at maximum speed he would be unable to take-off. An approach to give maximum lift would be too slow to give any horizontal distance. Hence the compromise in favour of speed.

This is an event which appeals to the naturally gifted: those who have speed and power. It would be true to say that all long jumpers could be sprinters; the reverse would seldom apply.

Long Jump

Fig. 56 Barbara Barrett (Great Britain) taken during an indoor international.

The success of a long jump is determined at take-off and nothing can be done in the air to increase the flight range. History indicates that the professional jumpers of the late nineteenth century, and those of the ancient Games, carried hand weights which they released at the apex of the jump, so changing the flight curve. Modern rules now prevent this.

'Lift' after a fast approach run, is gained by the execution of certain, precise movements at great speed. This picture shows an essential part of the event: a high pick-up of the free knee, together with a balancing movement from the opposite arm, as the athlete runs up off the narrow (8 in. [20 cm] wide) take-off board.

Indoor athletics is now a popular part of the track and field scene with yearly European Championships.

Long Jump

Fig. 57 Heide Rosendahl (West Germany) winning the long jump in the 1972 Olympic Games. Heide is recognised as one of the greatest all-round athletes of this era. She was narrowly beaten in the pentathlon by Mary Peters (figs 71 and 78).

Balance in the air is an important aspect of long jumping. The tendency for the body to rotate forwards once it is air-borne has to be controlled. To reduce this tendency, athletes perform a 'hitch kick' (leg cycling action) or a 'hang', before they prepare for landing. In simple terms, a 'thin shape' at the apex of the jump is required.

Fig. 55 shows Randy Williams soon after the apex of the jump. An essential feature of the pre-landing phase is well illustrated by this picture. The legs must be as far in front of the body as possible before they strike the sand.

A

B

C

D

Figs 58a–f The somersault style of long jumping demonstrated by John Delamere (U.S.A.).

In 1975, the I.A.A.F., in their wisdom, banned this style of jumping. The decision was criticised on the grounds that the style was similar to the Fosbury style of high jumping. However, in jumping for height the area can be raised and made soft but this would be impossible for the long jump event. Quite rightly, the sport must protect its participants as well as the spectators (ref. rotational javelin throw of Erasquin, Spain in 1950s).

This style encourages the rotation referred to in association with fig. 57.

E

F

Triple Jump

Fig. 59 Viktor Saneyev (U.S.S.R.) Olympic champion 1968/72, world record holder, in mid-air probably during the second phase of the jump.

It is hard to understand how an event such as this found its way into the track and field programme, as it is really a series of jumps. It is of fairly recent origin and was probably a British rural sport. Leaping, composed of a wide variety of bounding activities, captured the interests of the professional jumpers during the 1800s. The competitions, usually held close to public houses, attracted gambling and side stakes etc.

As the event has developed technically, so too has its name changed. It has been referred to as 'hop-skip-jump' and 'hop-step-jump', both suggesting a short middle phase. The modern term, triple jump, indicates that the event has three almost equal phases.

Triple Jump

Fig. 60 One of the few athletes of international status from India, Mohinder Singh Gill.

The problem facing the triple jumper is one of conserving speed over three successive phases. Contact with the ground could form a possible braking force as well as a propulsive one. The contorted shape, which jumpers assume in the air, is an aid to making each contact 'active'. Forward speed, on landing, can be enhanced by transferring momentum from a free limb to the body as a whole. Hence the 'split' of the thighs, well illustrated in this figure and the previous one.

As in all technical events, balance is a key feature. A flat-footed landing offers greater stability than a toe landing. Singh Gill seems to be anticipating the former.

Triple Jump

Fig. 61 Nelson Prudencio (Brazil) silver medallist in the 1968 and bronze medallist in the 1972 Olympic Games, about to take-off for the final phase.

It is interesting to note that the winner of the 1948/52 Olympic triple jump, A. Ferriera da Silva, and the most recent world record holder, Joao Carlos Oliveira, are Brazilian. Could heredity and environment be influential here?

In the 1968 Olympic competition the world record was bettered nine times and the first seven all broke the existing Olympic record. The most recent improvement, by Oliveira, of almost 45 cm ($1\frac{1}{2}$ ft) was also in Mexico City. The rarefied atmosphere would seem to have a dramatic effect.

Triple Jump

Fig. 62 This magnificent action shot is of Michal Joachimowski (Poland) landing in the sand after a triple jump.

When measuring a long jump, the official stretches the tape from the near edge of the take-off board to the point of contact in the pit closest to the board. If, in falling backwards, any part of the body touches the ground outside the pit then the jump is illegal. But a jump is legal if the same is done in a forward direction. The pit should measure at least 30 ft in length.

Pole Vault

Fig. 63 A superb fish-eye photograph of the pole vault.

This is the most spectacular of all events. In successive Olympics it has kept a packed stadium enthralled long after all the other events of the day have closed. Vaulting, like high jumping, is a competition of 'survival of the fittest' as, in theory, the number of attempts is unlimited.

The history of the event suggests that it developed, simultaneously, along two different lines, in different parts of England. In the Fenlands, concentration was upon distance, in order to clear the dykes and ditches, while the development for height was in the border counties, particularly Cumberland.

Technology has also been influential. Raised landing areas have been introduced, poles have changed from hickory to bamboo to alloy and finally to the fibre-glass poles in use today.

Pole Vault

Fig. 64 Wolfgang Nordwig (East Germany) reigning Olympic champion. Vaulters are very like the knights of the tournament, charging down the runway. Then they direct the end of the pole into a trough-like box and are catapulted into space.

The height of a vault depends upon the effective height at which the vaulter can grip the pole and still make it give vertical lift. The length of the pole is governed by rules, the height of the vaulter's grip by speed, stature, strength and his ability to execute aerial skills.

Pole Vault

Fig. 65 Jan Johnson (U.S.A.) on the way to clearing 5 m 20 cm (17 ft 0 in.). The 'glass' pole is charged with energy put there by the skill of the vaulter during the plant and take-off, conserved during the early flight, and finally returned to the vaulter when he needs it to clear the bar. The bend shows that Jan has put energy into the pole, his expression suggests that he is fighting to conserve it.

With a rigid pole it was possible literally to climb up it, as did the Ulveston Climbers of the 1880s: a group of men who forced the rule change now essential for modern pole vaulters. The top hand must remain firm, a feature so well illustrated by this picture.

Fig. 66 Chris Papanikolaou (Greece) in a bird-like pose,
fulfilling man's early dreams of unaided flight.

Fig. 67 Anatoliy Bondarchuk (U.S.S.R.) Olympic Champion and a world record holder. Bondarchuk, a significant name for a hammer thrower, has just set the hammer in motion before gyrating three times and finally releasing it high over the shoulders.

History links this event with royalty. Henry VIII of England, was keen on casting the 'barre'. The 'barre' is now a 7·257 kg (16 lb) ball on the end of a wire, the total length of which must not exceed 121 cms (4 ft).

Fig. 68 Valentin Dmitrenko, yet another skilful thrower from Russia.

Dmitrenko is pictured here during what is known as the 'single support phase', and shows the fine balance required for this event. To throw the hammer a long way, it is necessary to turn fast and keep the radius long. Turning fast requires balance, a feature superbly shown here, and the arms are stretched, thus keeping a maximum radius.

Fig. 69 Howard Payne, 1975 World Masters champion, reached the peak of a long international career when over 40 years of age. Together with his wife, Rosemary, they form one of the most famous partnerships in the sport.

Howard, shown here during the second of three turns, finds this sufficient to contain within the 2·135 m (7 ft) circle. Some world-class throwers use four turns.

Decathlon

Fig. 70 Bruce Jenner (U.S.A.) current world record holder with 8,524 points.

The decathlon is the true test of the all-round athlete. The ten events, listed on page 16, are spaced over two days. Each performance is timed or measured and then awarded a number of points, the total of which decides the result of the competition.

The decathlon was first introduced in the Olympic Games of 1912 when the event was won by the legendary Jim Thorpe. However, Jim, an American Indian, never received the honour of an Olympic champion because it was found subsequently that he had broken the amateur code. Jim continued in sport as a baseball player and footballer of some note.

Pentathlon

Fig. 71 A delighted Mary Peters (Great Britain) is about to receive the gold medal for winning the 1972 Olympic pentathlon. Mary beat the favourite, Heide Rosendahl (figs 57/78) by a mere ten points. This represents about 1 cm in the high jump or one tenth of a second in the 200 metres.

The pentathlon (the events are listed on page 16), is supposed to be the equivalent of the decathlon. As a test of all-round ability it falls well short.

It was first introduced to the Games of 1964, when Mary Peters was fourth and Mary Rand (fig. 81) was second.

Fig. 72 (*below*) The 1974 English schools championships. This is a very large meeting, identical in many respects to the Olympic Games, complete with the oath swearing ceremony and the parade of competitors. England has probably the most elaborate structure for schools' athletics in the world, but its competitions favour the precocious and many drop out of the sport before they mature. However, athletes like Anne Packer (1964 Olympic 800 metres) and Sheila Sherwood (1968 Olympic long jump) successfully made the transition to adult competition.

Fig. 73 (*opposite*) The final of the womens' 800 metres in the 1970 European junior championships. Waltrand Pohland (East Germany) beats Sylvia Schenk (West Germany). Such a championship is very new to the sport and is an ideal place to 'blood' future Olympic Champions. The European Junior Champions of today will very likely be the Olympic Champions of tomorrow.

Historical Landmarks

Fig. 74 (*below*) Dr. Roger Bannister makes a presentation to the sport of gymnastics.

Probably the greatest moment in British Athletics came on the evening of May 6th, 1954 when this man became the first person to break the barrier of the 4 minute mile. Metrication has taken away much of the intense interest associated with the mile. The time recorded by Bannister of 3 mins 59·4 secs, only remained a world record for one month. The subsequent twenty-one years have seen a further eight seconds lopped off it.

Fig. 75 (*opposite*) A unique photograph. David Hemery No. 12 and John Akii-Bua No. 23 have both won Olympic titles in the 400 metres hurdles, with new world records. They are truly world champions.

The only other Englishman to win this event was Lord Burghley, in 1928. It was a fitting tribute to Lord Burghley, a loyal supporter of the Olympic ideal, when he was invited to present the gold medal to David Hemery in Mexico City.

John Akii-Bua, in winning the event in 1972, became Uganda's first ever gold medallist in track and field.

Political Intervention

Fig. 76 Taken during an international presentation, the Russian athlete is bewildered by the raised, clenched fist. This protest, identical to that after the final of the 200 metres for men in 1968, is symbolic of the 'black power' group.

True sportsmen only wish to compete against the best in the world, a situation no longer possible because of differing political ideals.

Fig. 77 Esther Shakhamorov (Israel). Many will accept this as just another picture of a hurdler, but the truly initiated must certainly recognise the political undertones of the selection.

Esther qualified for the semi-finals of the hurdles event for women at the Munich Olympic Games and was their only world-class athlete. However, on the day her lane remained empty because, in the period between qualifying and having to race again, the 'Munich Disaster' took place.

During the early hours of September 6th 1974, extremists of the revolutionary Arab movement broke into the Olympic village, killed a member of the Israeli team, and held several others hostage in the team's quarters. By the end of the day, several other members of the Israeli team had been killed, including Amitsur Shapira the team's athletics coach, as a result of the subsequent disaster at the Munich airport. During the deliberations of the day, which included attempts to negotiate with the terrorists, the Israeli government demanded that the Games should be suspended immediately, but at 10.30 a.m. Avery Brundage, president of the I.O.C. announced that the Games would continue. Hence the movement, which had survived two world wars, was given another lease of life.

Success

Fig. 78 Heide Rosendahl, together with a team mate, are about to receive the gold medal for the 4 × 100 metres relay. This made a total of three medals for Heide in one Olympic Games (figs 57 and 71).

Success and failure have both caused the downfall of many athletes. Some find the notoriety of success beyond control, others find the prospects of failure frightening. Before this photograph was taken Heide experienced failure when eliminated from the pentathlon high jump at a height well below her capabilities. A mere 1 cm would have clinched another gold medal but Mary Peters (fig. 71) was experiencing the success this time, jumping higher than even the wildest dreams.

Success at an Olympic Games is sweeter when experienced by the host nation, as was the case in this picture. It offers some recompense for the vast sums of money spent in hosting the Games.

Tragedy

Fig. 79 One of the greatest tragedies I have seen in sport. Kerry O'Brien No. 25, from Australia, is about to take a plunge which eliminated him from the 1970 Commonwealth Games' steeplechase. As the world record holder at the time, he was clear favourite to win.

Nature –v– Nurture

Fig. 80 The relaxed sprinting style, associated with Negro athletes, of Ainsley Bennett (Great Britain). When one considers that the negro has almost completely dominated the sprinting events, it prompts one to ask — Is it nature or nurture? It is very doubtful if the negro has any inborn anthropometric attributes. However, the uncertainty of his environment, particularly in North America, could be a very big motivating force.

It must be admitted that a negro in full stride is an aesthetically pleasing sight.

Fig. 82   Mary and Samantha Toomey. Mary, the 1964 Olympic long jump gold medallist, is married to the talented all-rounder, Bill Toomey, the 1968 Olympic decathlon champion. Will Samantha follow in her parents' footsteps? Fig. 81 (*pages 140/141*) shows Mary as an athlete.

Careful breeding can produce a champion race horse. Is there any evidence to support a similar genetic factor in humans? Did Hitler attempt to breed the super race in Germany in the 1930s? If he did, as recent documentary films suggest, then could sport be reaping the benefit of this, only a generation removed? The German nations are certainly very powerful in sport at this moment.

Athletes in Training

Fig. 83 Judy Vernon (Great Britain) commonwealth hurdles champion, training with weights.

Strength is a prerequisite for all events. But the type of strength is specific to the event, and different methods are used for its final development. Weight training can provide the essential foundation upon which all other types of strength can be developed.

It is certain that one cannot become strong enough, for a power event, by just practising the event. Some form of progressive resistance must be used incorporating the overload principle. Here Judy is showing leg extension. The 'resistance' is the weighted discs and it can be made 'progressive' by adding more weights.

Fig. 84 (*pages 146/147*) Ian Stewart (Great Britain) training in his natural environment. Champions come from all sorts of localities. 'Lack of facilities' is an excuse for being idle.

Training is an act of faith. Good athletes train most days of the week, most weeks of the year, to prepare their bodies for the stress of competition. The type of training varies with the event: basically, the runner runs, the thrower lifts weights and throws, and the jumper bounds and sprints. But in all of them there is no short cut to success and there is no substitute for hard work.

Fig. 85 Lesley Kiernan, training in her local environment, which is in complete contrast to that of the previous figure.

This photograph might well illustrate the fact that athletes are made in the winter and merely blossom in the summer. Training is an investment account: the more one puts in, the more one can draw out at a future date. But the wise athlete consults a coach to make sure that the investment is sound.

Officialdom

Fig. 86 Retired headmaster, John Aspland, is about to start a 400 metres event. The microphone makes sure that all runners hear the commands. The pistol is linked to the electrical timing so that it can be set in motion with one action.

Sport cannot survive without the people who voluntarily administer it and direct its competitions. Their only reward is the enjoyment of others.

Fig. 87 A photo finish, together with a record of the timing, in the 4 × 100 metres in the 1970 Commonwealth Games. Using a straight edge one can determine that this race was won in 40·3 secs.

Electrical timings and photo finish results have certainly reduced the effect of human error in judging and timing running events. I am not so happy with electronic measurements in the field events. Like all athletes, I like to see the result on a tape measure.

Fig. 88 Alan Williams (Great Britain) at peak bend on the famed Catapole, the current leader in the race for pole superiority.

The technologist has certainly made the pole vault a rich nations sport. With the cost of a pole about £70 and a landing area as much as £1,000, poorer nations are being forced to abandon these events. Does sport really want this? If not, then the commercial exploitation of the sport should be controlled.

Fig. 89 (*pages 156/157*) The Apollogun javelin launcher, made by Accles and Pollock Limited, England, aids the design of the perfect javelin. When the javelin is in flight the resistive force is known as drag and the manufacturer is concerned with keeping this to a minimum. Experiments, using human throwers, are not precise enough for such research. The gun can reproduce the same launching conditions time after time.

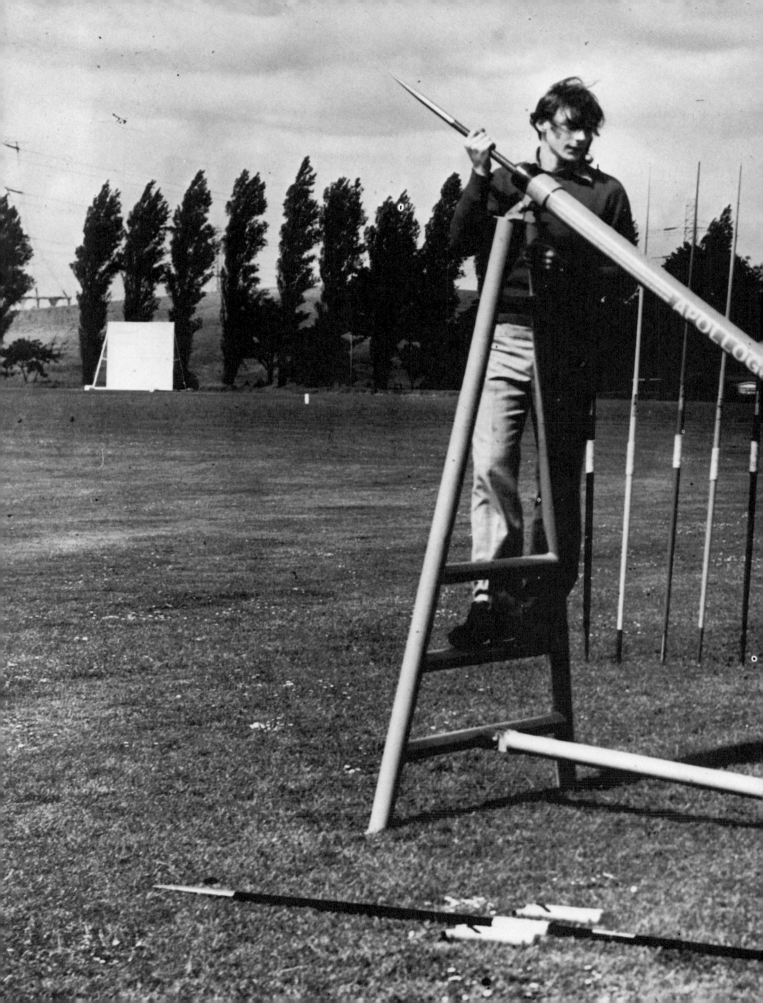

Commercialisation in Sport

Fig. 90 A photograph that could be of value to Cantabrian, the manufacturers of the blocks, or to Puma, the manufacturers of the shoes. Whether we like it or not, sport is big business. Business men are not philanthropists, they are in sport to make money, even if it means an athlete losing amateur status.

The progress of sport relies upon commercialisation, but uncontrolled it could bring about its downfall.

The Competition Arena

Fig. 91 (*pages 160/161*) A magnificent view of the 1972 Olympic stadium. The casual observer might notice the canopy and electronic scoreboard, but it is also a study of people and their response to success and failure.

The scoreboard confirms that Bondarchuk (U.S.S.R.) has won the hammer competition, while Uwe Beyer (West Germany), disappointed at finishing fourth, hides his face in his hands.

The Competition Arena

Fig. 92 A magnificent fish-eye view of the 1972 stadium silhouetting the Olympic tower, now essential for television, the elaborate stand canopy, an expensive luxury, together with the lavish stands and floodlighting. Such an extravaganza must raise the question — who can now afford the Olympic Games?